Date: 9/27/16

J 133.122 KOL
Kolpin, Molly.
Eerie haunted places /

Snap
books®

EERIE HAUNTED PLACES

BY MOLLY KOLPIN

Consultant:
Simon J. Bronner
Distinguished Professor of American Studies and Folklore
Chair, American Studies Program
Pennsylvania State University

CAPSTONE PRESS
a capstone imprint

Snap Books are published by Capstone Press,
1710 Roe Crest Drive, North Mankato, Minnesota 56003
www.capstonepub.com

Library of Congress Cataloging-in-Publication Data
Kolpin, Molly.
 Eerie haunted places / by Molly Kolpin.
 pages cm. — (Snap. Scared!)
 Includes bibliographical references and index.
 Summary: "Describes haunted places around the world"—
Provided by publisher.
 ISBN 978-1-4296-9980-8 (library binding)
 ISBN 978-1-4765-3558-6 (ebook PDF)
 1. Haunted places—Juvenile literature. I. Title.
 BF1461.K65 2014
 133.1'2—dc23
 2013001320

Editorial Credits

Mari Bolte, editor; Ashlee Suker, designer; Wanda Winch, media researcher;
Charmaine Whitman, production specialist

Photo Credits

Courtesy of Chuck Perry, 26; Courtesy of Joey Makalintal, 19; Courtesy of the Dorothy
Mackin Family, 15; Courtesy of Save our Heritage Organisation, 12; Dreamstime:
Lhalvorsen, 20, Ritu Jethani, cover, 1; iStockPhotos: anniegreenwood, 29; Newscom:
akg-images, 30, Picture History, 8; Photo provided courtesy of Alberta Culture, 25; San
Diego History Center, 13; Shutterstock: Anastasios Kandris, back cover, 4-5, c, 31, Can
Balcioglu, 22, David Nagy, 7, keren-seg, 2, 6, 14, 18, 24, 28, kropic1, 21, prudkov, 4-5
(background); U.S. Navy photo, 16; Winchester Mystery House, San Jose, CA, 9, 10 (all)

Design elements:

Shutterstock: basel 101658, tree branch silhouette, cluckva, stone wall design, David M.
Schrader, brush frame, Emelyanov, fractal pattern, foxie, brush stroke photo captions,
grivet, beige texture, happykanppy, black, green water color, HiSunnySky, grey grunge
frame, Igor Shikov, teal, purple frame, javarman, tree frame, cloud background, kanate,
olive water color, Leksus Tuss, green scratch texture, Massimo Saivezzo, grunge floral,
yellow, mcherevan, chandelier, NinaMalyna, ornate black frame, Nejron Photo, brown
wall texture, optimarc, line brush texture, pashabo, grunge brown, blue borders,
PeterPhoto123, smoke, Pixel 4 Images, trees section, Japanese calligraphic stroke, branch
design, Theeradech Sanin, distressed wood frame

Printed in the United States of America in North Mankato, Minnesota.
042014   008121R

Table of Contents

Who's There?

As you enter a dark building, you feel the hairs on the back of your neck prickle. Though you know you're alone, you have the eerie sense that someone—or something—is nearby. Suddenly, you hear a faint whisper. The whisper is followed by scuffling sounds. You catch a glimpse of a shadowy figure disappearing behind the doorway.

Was it a ghost? Is the building haunted? Ghostly,

mysterious events have been reported around the world.

You're about to step into some of the world's most haunted

places. Brace yourself, because things are about to get spooky!

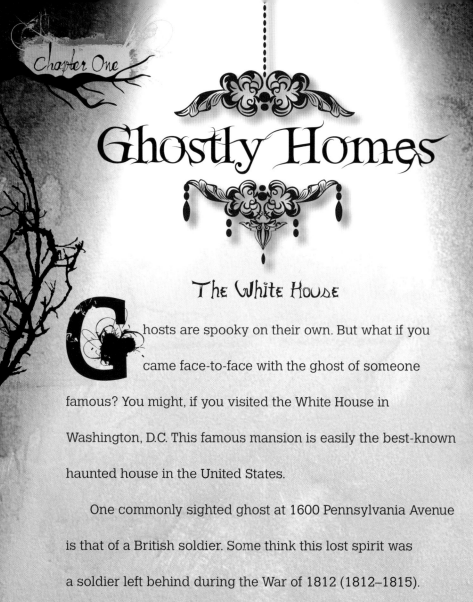

Chapter One

Ghostly Homes

The White House

Ghosts are spooky on their own. But what if you came face-to-face with the ghost of someone famous? You might, if you visited the White House in Washington, D.C. This famous mansion is easily the best-known haunted house in the United States.

One commonly sighted ghost at 1600 Pennsylvania Avenue is that of a British soldier. Some think this lost spirit was a soldier left behind during the War of 1812 (1812–1815). He has been seen walking across the front lawn. Some say that he always carries a lit torch.

President Franklin D. Roosevelt heard a ghost speak to him from the Yellow Oval Room.

The White House is the official home of the U.S. president and the president's family. But the current first family isn't the only one in residence. The ghost of former president Abraham Lincoln is said to show himself during times of trouble. His ghost was spotted frequently during World War II (1939–1945). First lady Eleanor Roosevelt, British Prime Minister Winston Churchill, and Queen Wilhelmina of the Netherlands all claimed to have seen Lincoln's ghost

A Family Affair

Abraham may not be the only Lincoln to haunt the White House. William Lincoln died of an illness during his father's presidency. After William's death, first lady Mary Lincoln claimed she would see her beloved son standing by her bedside each night.

Other former presidents and first ladies roaming the White House include Andrew Jackson and Abigail Adams. Andrew Jackson haunts the Rose Room, said to be one of the most haunted rooms in the White House. Abigail Adams' ghost can be seen hanging laundry near the East Room.

Many members of presidential families have seen or heard strange things in the White House. Both Hillary Rodham Clinton and Michelle Obama say they have felt something strange in the mansion. Could it be their imaginations? Or could they have sensed a ghost?

Winchester House

The White House reigns supreme as the east coast's largest haunted home. But the west coast has its own claim to fame—Winchester House.

In the early 1880s, Sarah Winchester visited a person who claimed to communicate with the dead. She wanted to speak with her husband, William, who had recently passed away.

At the time, a regular home could be built for around $1,000. Sarah spent $5.5 million on the Winchester House.

The psychic claimed to speak with William. His ghost said that the family was cursed by people killed by Winchester rifles. She needed to build a house in the west for the rifle victims. And for her safety, she could never stop building.

Spooky but True

Winchester House has 160 rooms, 2,000 doors, and 10,000 windows. There are six kitchens, 47 fireplaces, and 47 stairways. In all, the mansion sprawls over an area of 6 acres (2.4 hectares.)

The house is a maze of hallways. Stairs lead nowhere. Doors open into brick walls. Secret passageways are found in the walls. Sarah reportedly said the home's strange layout was meant to confuse unfriendly ghosts. However, the home has only a few mirrors. Sarah believed that spirits hated mirrors, and she wanted to keep friendly ghosts happy.

Sarah followed the ghost's advice. She bought a farmhouse near San Jose, California. She hired men to work on the house constantly. They worked around the clock, on weekends and holidays. Building continued for 38 years, until Sarah's death in 1922.

Visitors to Winchester House have heard footsteps and murmuring voices. People have felt cold spots inside the home. Some claim to have seen the ghosts of workers and servants.

Even Sarah may haunt the house. Some claim her presence is the strongest in the room where she died. During one visit, a psychic felt a great amount of pain and fell to the ground. Those around her said her appearance seemed to change to that of an older woman. Later she said she had felt the presence of "an overpowering woman." After all these years, Winchester House may really be a home for the dead.

Whaley House, 1865

Whaley House

From the outside, the Whaley House in San Diego, California, looks like any old two-story, brick-sided home. The home was built in 1857 on land once used as a place to punish criminals. With this kind of history, it's no wonder Whaley House has been called the most haunted house in the United States.

The home's most commonly sighted spirits are those of the original homeowners. Visitors have reported seeing the ghosts of Thomas and Anna Whaley walking down the house's stairway. Some claim they've also seen one or both of the Whaleys wandering the home's hallways.

Other strange occurrences have been reported as well. Windows sometimes open and close by themselves. Alarms go off for no reason. People have also experienced strong scents of tobacco and perfume.

The Whaleys are not the only spirits who live there. In fact, even Thomas Whaley believed the home was haunted. During his lifetime, Thomas often claimed to hear heavy boots clunking throughout the house. He believed these noises were made by the spirit of "Yankee Jim" Robinson. Yankee Jim was hanged on the Whaley House land before the house was built. Perhaps Yankee Jim encouraged the Whaleys to return to their home after death.

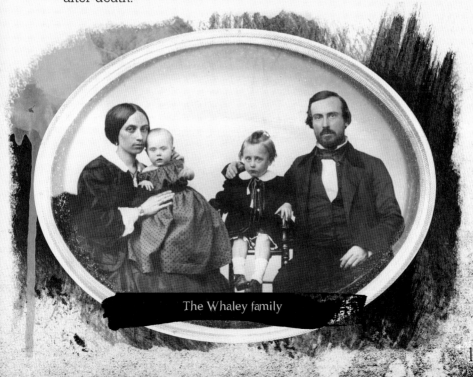

The Whaley family

Chapter Two

Haunted Hotels

Imperial Casino Hotel

George Long owned and operated the Imperial Hotel. But he never imagined that he'd be living there for eternity.

In 1890 gold was found in Cripple Creek, Colorado. The Collins Hotel was built in 1896 to house gold seekers and fame hunters. In the early 1900s English immigrant George Long bought the hotel. He and his family lived in an apartment next to the hotel's lobby. However, his daughter, Alice, suffered from an illness that caused her to become upset and violent. Her parents began locking her in the apartment to keep her away from the hotel guests.

One day in the late 1930s, George fell down a flight of stairs. Rumors flew that Alice had killed her father by hitting him on the head with an iron skillet. Nobody knows what really happened.

George died but he did not disappear. To this day, he continues to watch over the hotel. His ghost has been seen standing behind the hotel bar. George is also thought to be the cause of many other strange happenings at Imperial Hotel. Dresser drawers open on their own. Faucets turn on and off. But Alice may be there too. Visitors have heard scratching noises behind the door where Alice was kept.

When the hotel added a casino, the strange events only increased. One slot machine started spewing out coins. Other machines have made "dinging" sounds even when no one was using them. Could George or Alice's ghosts be behind the mysteries?

The hotel was renamed the Imperial Casino Hotel in 1914.

The Queen Mary

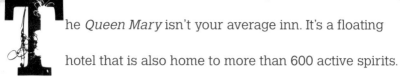

The *Queen Mary* isn't your average inn. It's a floating hotel that is also home to more than 600 active spirits. Many passengers have seen ghostly figures wandering the ship in old-fashioned clothing.

Now permanently docked in California, the *Queen Mary* can't escape its past. This former warship carried more than 765,000 soldiers during World War II (1939–1945).

The *Queen Mary* is also known as the "Gray Ghost."

Many sailors died onboard, from overheating to suicide to accidents on the water. Although their bodies are gone, their spirits may never have left the ship. People have heard strange thumps, bumps, and even screams while aboard.

The swimming pool area is one of the most haunted places on the ship. Some paranormal experts claim the area is a vortex to the spirit world. The vortex allows spirits to come and go as they please. One of the most famous pool ghosts is Jackie, a former passenger. The young girl is said to have drowned in a swimming pool. Jackie often appears for psychics and even interacts with tourists.

The Green Room is home to a ghost called "John Henry." He was a boiler room worker who was crushed to death while fleeing a fire. His body was found trapped in the ship's hull. Ghost hunters have seen shadowy figures in the room. They have also heard banging noises against the walls, and felt intense pressure on their bodies. With all these spirits hitching a ride, the Gray Ghost is truly a haunted houseboat.

Chapter Three

Paranormal Prisons

Eastern State Penitentiary

Dark prisons filled with dangerous criminals are scary enough. But what if you added ghosts to the mix? Eastern State Penitentiary is a former prison in Pennsylvania. Built 170 years ago, this building is now recognized as one of America's most haunted places.

This huge building was the world's first penitentiary. At the time it was built, prisons were nothing more than walls that kept prisoners in. Criminals found guilty of minor crimes were locked up with murderers. Men were locked up with women and children. Guards could punish prisoners cruelly.

Eastern State Penitentiary was once the largest prison in the world. It was also the most expensive to build.

In 1829 a new kind of prison opened its doors. At Eastern State Penitentiary, prisoners would not have to fear punishment from guards. They would receive better treatment. But they would also be locked in cells and away from other people.

In 1929 well-known gangster Al Capone was housed at Eastern State Penitentiary. Al claimed a spirit named Jimmy haunted him inside the prison. Jimmy had been one of Al's victims during the St. Valentine's Day massacre. Other prisoners said they heard Al begging Jimmy to leave him alone. Eventually the most feared gangster of the time lost his mind.

Each prisoner got his or her own cell. Every cell had heat and indoor plumbing, uncommon during that time. But there were no lights inside. The only light came from a small window near the ceiling, called a skylight.

Today the prison draws tourists from around the world. Many visitors have experienced activity inside the prison. Cell Block 12 is where many of the strange happenings take place. Tourists have heard laughter and spotted shadowy figures in the hallways. Some have even seen an odd mist floating out of the cells. Perhaps some of the building's former prisoners never managed to escape this haunted place.

He Had His Revenge

Al Capone may not have liked being haunted, but that didn't stop him from becoming a ghost himself! Five years after his stay at Eastern State, Al was sent to Alcatraz Island. Visitors to Alcatraz swear they can hear Al Capone playing his banjo in the prison showers.

Alcatraz

Alcatraz looks like an old, decayed stone castle. Fog often rolls over the rocky island in San Francisco Bay. The 160-year-old prison held kidnappers, robbers, and murderers. Although it hasn't had prisoners since 1963, some people believe ghosts remain locked within the prison's walls.

Alcatraz served as a federal prison from 1934 to 1963.

Difficult prisoners from all over the country were brought to Alcatraz.

Numerous visitors have heard screams, crying, and clanking chains. The sounds may belong to former prisoners who never left the island.

In 1946 three prisoners tried to escape. They ran down a hallway but were killed by gunfire and grenades. Today a large steel door covers the hallway. People say they have heard gunfire, shouting, moaning, and explosions coming from behind the door.

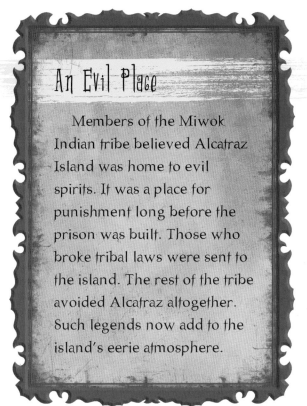

An Evil Place

Members of the Miwok Indian tribe believed Alcatraz Island was home to evil spirits. It was a place for punishment long before the prison was built. Those who broke tribal laws were sent to the island. The rest of the tribe avoided Alcatraz altogether. Such legends now add to the island's eerie atmosphere.

Alcatraz's Cell Block D is known for being especially haunted. Strange voices have been heard coming from cells 11, 12, and 13. Cell 14 is claimed to be cold no matter what the temperature is elsewhere. Many visitors to cell 14 have also reported a rush of sudden, powerful emotion. Could it have been their imagination? Or are these feelings caused by a tormented soul locked up forever in Alcatraz's spookiest cell?

Chapter Four

Stage Fright

Empress Theatre

When the curtains close after a show, most take this as their cue to leave. But not everyone gets the message. Theaters are popular resting grounds for ghosts. Because cast and crew spend so much time there, theater ghosts may even get a name. The Empress Theatre in Fort Macleod, Alberta, Canada, is said to have a permanent visitor named Ed.

People describe Ed as an old man with hairy arms. In life, Ed may have been a janitor at the theater. Children have spotted Ed standing behind them in mirrors. Actors on stage have seen Ed sitting in the crowd during shows.

The Empress is Alberta's oldest theater.

One actor claimed he was alone at the theater one day during lunch. Eager to explore, he went into the basement and wandered into a dark room. Suddenly, he heard laughter. The room's door slammed shut behind him.

When the other actors returned to the theater, they found their friend. The actors had all been at lunch together. None of them could have played the prank. The trickster, it seemed, had vanished like a ghost. Perhaps Ed appeared, wanting to bring some drama to life.

The Hibbing High School ghost's favorite seat is J47.

Hibbing High School

Built in the 1920s, Hibbing High School is a large, castlelike school in northern Minnesota. The school's theater is thought to be haunted. The resident ghost seems to like watching the performances.

The ghost has even been caught on film. A photo taken in 2000 shows him as a hazy figure in a top hat. Some believe him to be the ghost of the theater's first stage manager, Bill.

Bill was well known among local residents even before he was photographed. In the 1970s, a girl was preparing for a performance in one of the auditorium's dressing rooms. She saw a man come into the room. When she turned to look at him, he disappeared. Was this man simply a stranger who had walked into the wrong room? Or had the actress caught a glimpse of the famous Hibbing High School ghost?

The Forever Encore

Theaters have many traditions about ghosts. One tradition calls for the theater to be closed one night a week. This is so the theater ghosts can put on their own productions.

Other theaters leave a single light on after everyone has gone home. This light is called a ghost light. Some think the lights are there to help ghosts put on their own plays. Other people believe the lights keep ghosts away.

Chapter Five

Spirits Overseas

Paris Catacombs

Ghosts in a building are frightening enough. But ghosts prowling below ground may be even more terrifying. The Paris Catacombs, a network of tunnels beneath the city, rank among the world's most haunted places.

In the late 1700s, Paris cemeteries became overcrowded. The city's cemeteries were closed. The bones from those cemeteries were moved to the catacombs. Today these tomblike tunnels hold the skeletons of more than 6 million former yet forever Parisians.

The Paris Catacombs are open to visitors. Brave individuals can walk through the dark, winding tunnels and see the millions of bones packed inside. It's no surprise that such a grim place is said to be haunted. Some visitors have heard strange voices. Others have seen spooky shadows moving along the tunnel walls. Perhaps these visitors are simply letting their imaginations run wild. Or maybe spirits really do live among the bones of the dead.

The catacombs stretch nearly 200 miles (320 kilometers) under the city of Paris.

Tower of London

The Tower of London is often considered the most haunted place on Earth. Construction on the tower began in the early 1080s. For the next 900 years it was used as a castle, a fortress, and a prison. Today its claim to fame is its many ghosts.

Two of the Tower's most famous ghosts have royal bloodlines. In 1483 12-year-old King Edward V and his younger brother Richard, the Duke of York, were mysteriously murdered. Their bodies were hidden in the Tower.

Edward (left) and Richard in the Tower

The Tower was used as a zoo, a prison, a fortress, and a torture site.

The skeletons of the princes were found in 1674. But some believe their restless spirits continue to wander the dark tower hallways. The Princes in the Tower often appear in front of visitors wearing white nightgowns and holding hands.

Along with these royal brothers, other ghosts may haunt the Tower of London. Some visitors have felt as though they were being crushed or strangled. Others have been pushed out of rooms. Many have reported hearing voices.

One thing is for sure: The boundaries between life and death have been tested. Whether these places are truly haunted or not is up to you to decide.

READ MORE

Chandler, Matt. *The World's Most Haunted Places.*
The Ghost Files. Mankato, Minn.: Capstone Press, 2012.

Everett, J. H. *Haunted Histories: Creepy Castles, Dark
Dungeons, and Powerful Palaces.* Christy Ottaviano Books.
New York: Henry Holt and Company, 2012.

Stone, Adam. *Haunted Houses.* The Unexplained. Minneapolis,
Minn.: Bellwether Media, Inc., 2011.

INTERNET SITES

FactHound offers a safe, fun way to find Internet sites related to
this book. All of the sites on FactHound have been researched
by our staff.

Here's all you do:

Visit *www.facthound.com*

Type in this code: 9781429699808

Check out projects, games and lots more at
www.capstonekids.com

OTHER TITLES IN THIS SET: